ELUSIVE LIFE

ELUSIVE LIFE

A book of poems

By

MILAFLOR GARCIA BARRERA NAVARRO

2017

ISBN : 978-0-9858770-4-0

DEDICATION

I lovingly dedicate this book to my beloved father Marceliano Batchar Barrera and to my sweet and loving mother Albina Garcia Barrera. May they look down on my poetry.

However, what really gave me a head start in writing poetry and later encouraged me to publish it is no other than the man I ever loved, Dr. Nicanor J. Navarro (Manuel Lasso).

FOREWORD

I have been requested to make a prologue for this book. Although I might be the less indicated person to perform such a delicate task I have accepted with delight because its reading illuminated me.

Its author is by birth, a native of the *Pearl of the Orient Sea*, the Philippines, and by self-education, a poet. It might be more accurate to say, a born poet, refined by self-cultivation.

These poems have to do with the sufferings the poet had to endure during her entire life.

In a very impressive way this book deals with Death and Love. Death, the eternal antagonist of humans and Love, the constant motive on their pristine happiness. Love is dealt in all its forms. There is love towards her father from whom she remembers his moments of drunkenness and the instants when he showed his affection for her. The author also deals with the love for her husband, her beloved Nicanor, who shared her romantic ecstasy with proportional intensity. Equally moving are the remembrances of her love towards her children.

There are poems based on her tragic experiences during the Japanese invasion of her land, the abuses committed against the civilian population and the family members interactions which left on her painful memories.

In short this author has spoken about her own mortality and her own pure capacity to love, describing the pain and miseries of her adulthood counterbalanced with the joys of her existence with a marvelous poetic artistry.

You are invited to participate in an artistic feasting of poems and images which will leave you wishing to read more.

Congratulations to this new carver of the word and to her marvelous book.

Manuel Lasso

TABLE OF CONTENTS

Don't Say Goodbye

Brother,
      don't say
        goodbye,
          Sorrows
            We felt,
              With signs
                Of guilt

For
    I can't say,
      I love
        you
          When
            you are
              gone!

REMISSION

Goodbye, oh beautiful life,

Nature rented when I was born

A loan, so short a term

To enjoy what was given.

The years in my childhood vanished

As I turn around, my brothers gone.

My beloved father perished,

To a mortgage he couldn't run.

Bless us, Oh! Heavenly Spirit,

As we live the life in temptations;

Bestow us light and permit

Our souls, in remission.

MY ETERNAL HOME

In my eternal home
I cannot rest
But, linger, to these lonesome years in solitude
Yet, with patience I do await.

Oh, my beloved, be strong
For your happiness, is my joy and peace
Your sorrows, my agony
Your sufferings, my lamentations.

Await, in our home with peace
To lie beside me, forever;
In our cold eternal haven.

Forever.........
And all eternity we will be in peace,
Waiting..........for

All our children to join us,
At the end, again,
We will be together,
A family,
    in peace!

NOTHING TO NOTHINGNESS

IF WE CAME FROM NOTHING,

IN NOTHINGNESS WE WILL END.

OUR LOVE AND LIFE WE HAVE LIVED

WILL BE THE MEMORIES OF THE LIVING.

WALLS OF INFINITE SECLUSION

Walls of infinite seclusion
Where I could pour my pain
And bury my sorrows..............
If, I who love, but can't be loved by anyone;
This life with countless sorrows
And yet, to live a hundred years
Of pain and anguish...............
How could I or how should I address
This world in my great disgrace;
I, who won't be remembered or cared
By people, whose love I shared;
Would be senseless thoughts
To go on living, to see the sky
With twinkling happy stars, and why,
Should a person live
To aspire to be loved
When no one could have
Given, nor think of giving
Precious is the life? When loomed
With bitterness and pain?
Ah, ha! At last I could live in peace
Inside these muted walls
Release my pain in isolation
My world....... in seclusion!

EPITAPH

LAY A RED ROSE ON MY CHEST

TO LET ME KNOW YOUR LOVE EXISTS;

BUT NOT TO GRIEVE FOR MY SAKE

FOR THY SADNESS I CANNOT TAKE

NENENG

MY LIFE

My life so dull.....

No moon no star

The day so gloom.

The coming of storm.

MY DAY HAS COME

My day has come ....
They punched my chest, pinched my arms
And dug my veins to no avail.

I utter no complaints..........
To this torture that must be done!
Yet, desperate measures to no response.

I found myself.............
In a freezing lonely place,
Wrapped in white as lace.

This solemn day.........
Church bells clinging to my ears
Crowd of people pacing in tears.

Crickets songs...........
Filled my ears, in this darkened place,
The earthen smell adds to it's creepy mood.

SWEETER THAN HONEY DEW

I must go, I must go, to grandma, yes, I must
To sip her tuba, sweeter than honey dew.
The gatherer, the gatherer, tuba on his back
Overnight drippings, of tuba from the pulp.

She'd took a tiny glass
That fits my fingers through
Pour in that red, red tuba
Sweeter than honey dew.

This tipsy girl of two
Start dancing on the street
Joy of the grandma
To see her dancing feet.

Amused, not her father
Worried of his daughter,
Grow-up alcoholic
To the streets she'll frolic.

CLOUD OF DUST

I wait, for you, oh cloud of dust
To slap my face, make me aghast
I must and will, avoid your coming,
As you see me already running.

But you are most invincible
To my poor nose, who's gullible
And I'll be coughing, coughing like rain
That raise my pain up to my brain.

Hush, if only snow thus come today
For whole-year on the ground will stay,
No city streets with a cloud of dust
But slippery snow we hate to last.

DRUNKARD OF HIS TIME

What have you been drinking, if I may ask?

Your face reddened, looks abashed

Drink from morn 'til dusk

Your clouded eyes like frozen fish,

(To my dislike)

Staggering, "who wants to fight?",

Whoever made you drunk

I curse, that he is alive

Your dearest friend, my enemy

For what he does, defies our family.

TO NONOY DEMPS

TRACES OF YOUR SMILE

CREEP TO MY DULL MEMORIES

BUT LINGERS IN MY RESTLESS SOUL!

NENENG

SONGS FOR A FATHER

Songs for a father
Whose love and caring days are gone.
Songs, to his playful moods and how,
A big smile, and hug as I kiss thy brow;
Those strong knees, I lean on,
When family gathered around.
Uproarious songs, to that authoritarian voice?
Only, when behavior clashes his choice!

Easterly wind blows
Love songs, humming, whistling you hear
That gears to our happy atmosphere
As flowers bloom in the garden, he cares.

But now, where is that song?
Songs, for a father who's gone?
Never to be seen and be heard again?
Yet, it's blatant beneath my chest;
Whose anguish never ceased.
Dreams of him, I welcome in my sleep
To once more hear his songs, now so deep.
Tormenting moments to wake-up he's gone
Rejecting the knowledge where he lies
No more could I see, nor touch,
No more could I hear, his songs.

Songs for a father, in memories
Songs, he sang for me to sleep
Happy and love songs vibrates in my heart
And that soft voice, that calls my name.

No more songs, but memories remain............
That hurts like a thousand thorns;
To see the tombstone, I cannot bear
Nor think the six foot deep and four
Where he lies and can't sing no more.
The stone says, I can't see him no more,
And the songs, can't be heard no more.
Yes, oh, yes! No more songs, for years was ignored
No songs, no laughter,
No soft voice, that calls my name
Only the shiny stone remains............
In that lonely murky place, where darkness lurks.

DELIRIUM

My hands and feet were tied.
Shout of help, but no one comes
Attempts of escape I tried
A crazy clown I become.

I saw a snake sliding on my feet
Kicking and howling, I did so hard
While roaches crawling under my sheet
Two leopards standing guard.

Hooray! At last! An angel came
Ouch! The bee stung my arm
I feel my body getting numb
The angel in white, smiles like a charm.

I wake up tied and achy
A smiling nurse says good morning to me,
Breakfast in bed, looks funny
This lady in white, let my hands free.

MY FAMILY

I told my sister, that I'm mad
For I am a sinner on this earth.
I love my brothers, but too proud to admit
In my death, my heart, will bleed for it.

It hurts me deep when big brother got married
To a sister-in-law so wicked
She tells lies and me to blame
And light a fire, my brother's head to flame.
But, all that I could think and see
All my brothers love more of me
They asked me no questions
They knew me well with satisfaction.

(In our family), to repeat the scene or word is forbidden
Sealed our lips, secrets must be forgotten
To keep the house quiet in harmony
Mom's behind, holding the key.

DEEP THOUGHTS

Rolling my eyes up to the sky,
In count of three, I close them tight
Left arm so light, I raise it high
And feeling cold my toes like ice.

I fell, in happy thoughts so deep
Concentration on memories I keep,
Pain subdued by joy of past;
The ecstasy my heart could blast.

Nevertheless, the counting is back
Brain's, aware, the eyes crack
My toe so numb, in surgeon's hand
Surgery completed, I felt so grand.

MY FEAR

For all my days, I live in fear
That I might leave my children in tears
The thought of leaving is killing me
For time is now my enemy.

Even if Hecate drags me to that river
I'll fight with my faith and must be clever
For my soul and spirit's vow to thee
My sons and daughter waiting for me.

At night as I see them asleep
In their bed where they lie, I creep
Innocent faces smiles
What wicked heart, (to leave them) a mother could be so vile.

IF YOU MUST LEAVE ME

If you must leave me
Don't cease in coming to my side,
And let me feel your presence
In everyday of my life.

Your company I need in my struggle
With this life on earth I have to tackle.
No other ways to live but wish for you to stay
With me, in my cold bed for you to lay.

At night when I'm all alone
Remembrance of you I cherish more
To God I beg, to saints I implore
Bestow me strength, to bear it on.

HOW COULD I BE SO RIDICULOUS

How could I be so ridiculous?
To conceive without reflections
Ideas in my caked, disabled brain,
Who cogitate to change, what had past?

To my gripe, of what I have done
Abandoned, the helpless timid bull.
"Mercy....." uttered his purpled lips and fell
On the hard cemented floor.

Where was I, in his time of needs?
Away, in the distant soil, I fled
Self-reproof not present in my head
I bestowed him, my neglect, when I depart.
My ludicrousness unforgivable
Sufferings I ignore, for I deserved much more
The agony I cause, irretrievable
To my beloved father, I do honor.

PRISONER OF THE PAST

I am, of what I thought
Of what I feel
Of what I think
A prisoner of the past.

The past that shades pains
Agonies persist
Guilt contemplates
My perception repulsive.

I cried for freedom
From the past
That ruptured
My tormented heart.

IF DEATH WILL COME UPON ME

If death will come upon me,
Would I face it gallantly?
Or feel so cowardly
As any living soul does with?

For death could be so painful,
And it will be scary;
To fell, in the vacuum of darkness
Whose end, would never come!

How would I feel, if shadow comes
Or signs, it's coming to thee?
No words, could be uttered to describe my fear;
For sure, no happiness will fill the air.

To think I've lived my life in parables
The things I didn't understand, those troubles,
Questions, my life sought for answers
My consolation, I found only in dreams.
But now, the dreams of death lingers in my thoughts
So many a time prayer's has lost its power
Cyclone thoughts beneath my skull so strong
Like tidal waves that upon me, hovers.

Or so accept without regrets?

22

And to care not, of the living?
For I'll be blessed of no emotions in my tomb;
To see them cry or smile no meaning to my sight.

However, if death be shown so bright,
Who am I not to accept?
The fearless propositions of life
And be welcomed, by my long forgotten loved ones.

FOR ONLY I MUST DWELL

For only I must dwell..........
In this cold sepulcher,
Above my brother's door
Who lies on a cold marbled floor.
No need of tears, nor pity
For I must leave if not this way;
Be sooner my destiny.

Unfortunate, indeed, I grieve you all.
I felt no earthly pain
You looked down, and me so vain.

Whoever cause you this grief
Has caused its own
Though they've a heart of stone.

Damage was done,
By a heartless man
In the bright afternoon sun,
In two, my heart he sliced,
That staggered me, I cannot move
Nor utter words of my last good-bye.............

TOO LATE

My beloved sister
I did not forget
I left with no goodbyes
Was forced with no remorse
To this endless journey
With no company.
I'll be alone, I know I will
In this dark and gloomy trail
So sad, that I have to............
Choice, was not at hand
Chances, I ignored
Too late, too...... late,
Much, much, much... too late!

MY FAVORITE COLOR

Black, the color I love to wear,
Solemn and radiant to the air
To have them in me, makes me glee
With pride I feel every day.

Yet, not when mother says I must!
I wear them, the black with lust.
No glimpse of smile but tears inside
The law and custom, I have to abide.

To see a raven in the mirror
Clocked in black, face with horror
The pain so deep, creep in my heart
Agony I felt, my brother's depart.

PACIFIC WATER

Sitting on the rock by the water,
Away from the shack that clutters,
Overlooking the ocean so vast
With those creepy waves that move fast.

My heart ponders, to think you're yonder
Yearning for your love, that's so tender
Those painful thoughts, hoping to be well
Looking at the ocean, so calm and still.

We swim in Pacific water
Which currents and waves make it faster
Yet, unknown to each other
What Cupid plans to deliver.

Crashing sounds of waves upon the stones
Make my thoughts deeper to my bone.
Naive of what would be the future
My love, only in my thoughts, I nurture.

Shadowed by circumstances,
I wish for you be at my glance;
And not swimming in the beach of Peru,

While me here, feeling so blue.

To my great surprise, after a decade
We met each other by the cascade
While people lying half dead
You got your chance and took the lead.

Now, that we finally met
Away from the Pacific where my heart was set,
A few smiles and glances
We broke our silence and we took our chances.

CRY WITH NO TEARS

To cry with no tears,
On my cold and rigid face
To see them lock me, without embrace.
I cannot touch, nor be touched no more;
By my beloved NICANOR.

My heart's grieving, that I'm leaving
The one's life that's loving;
Now, a soundless, endless, cry.......
Had accepted, the given place without remorse
For graving does make it worse.

No glimpse of light
But darkened night
No tears that fall
And no one to call
Not even, my beloved NICANOR.

NOTORIOUS LOVE

Oh, notorious love, come to me
Wake-up, the sleepy heart of thee;
Whip and lash, if you may
So I could enkindle today.

Oh, notorious love, don't break my heart
That musical voice, you played to my ears,
Can't wait the day, again, I will hear
The songs of love, that dry my tears.

Oh, notorious love, what brings you to me,
This heart so meek, for years, now gone astray
Rambling like a bull, shouting "hooray".
To sip, the sweetness of love, from thee.

I WAS HURT

I was hurt
And so are you.
And our pride?
Shows, different view
We acted, opposite
To how we feel.
Feelings, uncontrolled
That distort our will.

AND WHEN THAT DARKENED NIGHT

And when that darkened night
The day said it's goodbye
My love, that I can't reach
For he was not in sight.

Tears flooded on my face
Voices, that love posses
Has endless tales
And lovers, asked its grace.

MY JOURNEY

My

journey

beyond,

May

be

lighter

if............,

I...............?

I

have

repented.............

my.........

sins.

AN INFANT, AM I?

I feel so tired,

My eyes won't open.

The path too narrow,

In my dark burrow.

The message I sent,

Was seriously challenged!

Rebellious was I, had revenged!

I shouted!, and was admired.

(Dedicated to my darling son MICHAEL)

OH! NATURE, WE COMMENCE OUR BEAUTY TO THEE

Oh, nature, we commence our beauty to thee
We kindly dispose, the showers in April's day;
That we can show our loveliness in May.
Lustrous roses clustered in the garden
Lilies and jasmine to thy grace it broaden;
To the center of our heart, sat a bumble bee,
Sucking our sweetness, to make its honey.

Rain drops that quench our thirst
In warm summer's noon.
The sun don't shine, nor does the moon!
The soft breeze of western wind
Blows our charm, and to the grass we bend
Spreading our splendor on the grassy floor
Disgrace we felt, upon our door.

To our loveliness, we thou compare,
A maiden, so dainty and fair.
Perfumed bosom, upon the break of day;
Frolicked by birds in days of May.
Sweet songs of nightingale that serenades
As darkness comes, the moon has shades
'til morning dusk, awaits for the climbing sun.

THAT PATIENT OF MINE

Limping as he walks,
Lamb-like, he talks.
Complains of pain he suffers
Money to pay, he can't offer.

Showed, the doctor his thigh,
Red, as raspberry pie.
Climbed-up, on the table he did,
Big pillow under his head.

Exposed his thigh to the air
So red, inflamed, he cannot bear.
For prescription was given,
Medicine, not taken!

GOODBYE BEAUTY

Goodbye beauty, how nice while you last
Praised and admired by people as I pass
Be it young, or old, has looked back
Though born poor, but beauty was her luck.
Hailed Princess, her father not a king,
Happy and playful, always in her swing.
Not a boring beauty, 'til she reached forty.
But beauty is not forever
That everyone should remember
Brief is our lives, so short it lasts.

Oh, beauty, beauty, beauty that passed
Like a lark that sings at dark
Now my face like a tree bark
So wrinkled, like a paper crumpled.
Why beauty was given, so fast it's taken?
Why'd you bake, then smashed your cake.
What then is life, that takes a gleam
And woke-up gone, or gave a shame.
With cabbage face, and crocked knees,
No princely lips, would plant a kiss
To this old, and wrinkled face
Just say ....goodbye........., beauty that has no trace.

FREEDOM?

Freedom.........................?
Which every being embrace,
Plants and grass with boundless growth
In those soils, fertile and vast,
Animals and birds in jungles move fast
For hunter's amusement, sought.
While rivers widely flow to meet the ocean's grace,
Nimbus, its immaculate beauty filled the sky
Gigantic forms drifting so high.

Freedom.............for the souls,
As death, the answer of defeat?
For those who rebel and failed?
In the land, the evils domain
The people were victims and were dupe.

Freedom..............to human minds,
That droves glory to decline.
Those glorious castles, had their moment,
Throne and power combined
In the forgetfulness of our time.

Freedom.............., we enjoy, yet, we suffer its fruits.
Violence in the streets, we deny its roots
Abuses of the rich, poor has to endure;

Criminals expect, people to concur,
Gratification to their vicious feat!

Freedom.................of thoughts
That Plato did his own,
Aristotle fell on his turn
Socrates gave his life;
While, Caesar, got a knife.
St Agustin had spoken,
Some laws were forsaken.
As Cervantes wrote Quixote,
Shakespeare made his big booty.

HORIZON

In the fields
Of battle, we cry
For God sake,
Why..........?

Brothers and foe,
Were killed.
Avenge of heart,
Thou healed!

Dragging limbs,
Limping, crawling,
As we move.
Horizon, we're told.

Sick, hunger and thirst
Walking in pain
Moaning, groaning you hear
Straight to horizon, we dare!

Half hidden sun,
Face of gold
Far, from reaching,
Yet, we uphold!

HOW COULD I FORGET

How could I forget..............
Those smiles that struck
Like lightning to my heart.

How could I forget..............
Your kisses, sweater than
Honey suckle sipped by bees.

How could I, forget..............
Your touch, that makes me weak
My spine, so cold I could not move.

And how, could I forget...........
That birdlike language upon your tongue,
Whispering, whispering....I love you!

How could I...............
How could.... I, forget..........
You....................

SO ALONE...........

So alone, as anyone could be
Playing in dunes, on summers day
May it morning or noon
I found myself, left alone..........

No playmates, no peers to play
In the fresh breath of morning breeze,
No footsteps, on the sand that I could trace,
But peace of my soul........, all I could get.
No morning waves, to greet me,
Miniature crabs, does run away.
I found myself alone, so alone, by the sea.

I turned around and face the ocean,
Those blue water so steel...., no commotion.
The skies so clear, no clouds on site
No seagulls flying, with the sun so bright,
Those trees unmoved, in its full height;
Bleak morning, and a chilly night.

I was alone, running in the pasture,
In spring's day, or summer's noon.
No stars at night, nor shine of the moon
No chirping birds, at the break of dawn.

CONVERSATION TO MIGRAINE

Headache? Where are you?
Why, you want to know?
This is my body!
And so?
You're disturbing, where are you?
Above you, dumb head!
Just, where in my head?
I don't know, am looking around.
Stop looking around, get out!
Don't be nasty, I want to rest.
You don't rest, you're rambling in my head!
Well, 'cause I am not comfortable.
Get out, leave, I want peace.
O.K., O.K......, why don't you sleep.
You're telling me? How?
You sleep........., I'll leave.
Fine! I'll see to that!
Bye.................?

I MISS THOSE MOMENTS

I miss those moments with you

When we used to share one for two

No motion of pain we feel

But happiness on our faces one could tell

The passion we felt of no compare

With flare of fire that was so rare

Scruples denied by heart so in love

That twine us like doves.

WHERE LOVE HAS GONE

For when a sharp knife passes through my heart with no relief
What more thy aching heart could bear,
Those pain that death could not erase;
But yet my soul longed for thy embrace?

In the steel dusk of dawn, that pain is even more,
As I laid awake the night before.
To think how sweet our love that past
Which mortals gloat those tenderness so untouched.
Now, shadowed with hate that last.

Where and how wronged began,
When our lives so contempt to one.
No need of dart which Cupid could have thrown,
Devised by Venus to herald her throne.
No passion could salvage the love that then was lost.

How will I hide those pains that dig within,
And all I see speaks of how I feel;
For sorrows demand attention and so it's known
As dying man so hide, but it is shown;
Its remorseful face that glooms with pain.

CRIES OF PEACE

The fools, the victim, and the pitiful;
Avenge their pain of lunacy,
A strong politics in the neighborhood that dwells
In the songs of the forbidden, forgotten souls.

Alleluia, to the hierarchy that leads
In the absurdity of men, that was created.
No tears, no sobs, no fortitude
In the land of lunatics appears.

Cries, of bitterness could be heard
Reaches Olympus as it may be concealed
No remedies, no sublimation as it was told,
By thy creator who thus behold!

Yet, in the tempestuous cities of sinners,
Rise the questions no one could answer
But hide their crimes, shame and infidelity
And crowned themselves as conquerors of society.

"Peace be with you", cried the Priest,
But where does peace loom, in the quest
Of the river Styx, a dreadful journey
Where lunacy has to end; and where Hades holds the rein!

Repentance, then so acclaimed
By those souls with endless pain
Too late, too… late for the souls to blame
Thyself, whose journey has no end.

UNFORTUNATE ME

In capabilities thus me deceive

In my strong and youthful stage

Now, where are those arms and legs?

Whose work has left no trace?

But of pain, anguish and miseries!

Rise, where you have fallen;

But not to be forgotten

That pain thus come again.

Let out a smile on your face,

To hide the pain of disgrace.

No warmly arms to thee, embrace

No fame, no beauty, no love.......

But sorrows..........for the unfortunate me.

Yes.........., the unfortunate, unfortunate me.

ST. ROSE OF LIMA

And in my sleep the night I couldn't rest,

You woke me up with smile on your face

A maiden by the well, with beauty like lace

Dressed in chiffon, that covers its best.

Could it be a dream, or am I dreaming.

Smell of roses that blossoms in May

Classic beauty, cattleya has its say,

Envious with the wind, to my dismay.

If it's a miracle, which I needed most,

All the sufferings, man couldn't hold

Bow thy head to thee, for thy noble name we behold,

And say an ardent prayer when I am lost.

TIME OF REGRETS

Mother, do forgive me............?
Life not easy, now, I know
I did and what I did, was wrong, I see
Grieve not, for thee, my heart's low.

Forgive, for the things I've done
The hard way, I do, now learned
Pains, in thine heart well soon be gone,
If thy forgiveness, I then, have earned.

Melancholic is my heart, not seeing you,
You live in a land so far away
I disgrace thee with my virtues,
Imploring, for second chance, if I may?

To thee, I owe my life, my soul!
Repaid with hideous torments of shame,
I did so bad, I didn't reach my goal;
Lost the game, in shame, and I'm to blame!

But yet my hopes not lost,
With courage, I'll fight my battle
Battalions of sons, daughters and wife, I boast
Bullets of hopes, and love will rattle!

A SONNET TO NICANOR

Nicanor, the name that I adore.

Left me in pain, to my great vain

He went hunting, of the meat so lean,

The courage he took not when he spoke.

To this distant land, he will explore;

And bear those pain, as he's provoke

Non-gentlefolk's, to thee, he looked

My Nicanor, the man that I adore.

He sat down, to the desk he found

A note of love, he smiled with pleasure

Catch his eyes........ the red rose on the ground

Sweet smile on his lips, for he was sure

He's the man that I adore.

With fruits of love, we cherished forevermore.

SPRING

Spring......, the most welcome of all

As winter coming to its fall.

Whose reign of power so long

In its bad mood it gets strong.

Spring, Spring, Spring........we love Spring.

And who doesn't love Spring?

March ends so fast,

Traces of snow didn't last.

The flowers, the grass, the trees

Greeted by the buzzing bees.

Rising sun welcome's with smile

April shower's blessed the flowers with guile.

LAMENTING HEART

If someday we meet
White hairs on our heads
The words you seek
My mouth won't speak
But does my tears.
My lips tied, thy name for years
Your eyes hunts strength of sorrow
Unfeeling heart languish in morrows.

We've parted, silence filled the air
No goodbyes said, but flood of tears
Thy face loomed, in my head for years
Thy emotions, in despair.
Your kisses beseeched me, in my sleep
Spears of pain, bores my heart so deep
No regrets of moments, now's a dream
We've shared splendor, of the lost game.

You're proud, not to my shame
Avoided its other, to which we grieve
For our convictions, moments deceive
Our hearts broken, and I was blamed.
The pain in years not vanished by time
Clouded mind, never could shine
Alluring kisses, I once adore
Was my knell to Hades door.

THE GRIEVING LOVE

If I must go, and you to stay
Don't lay me into the ground
That humid mist I cannot endure
For I, may not see the sun, that, I do assure
Yet, to think how hopeless one could be,

Be buried for eternity
Though, everything has always a way
However, your thoughtfulness will give my wish
A red, red rose be planted on my chest
To let thee know thy love's blessed
For thy love leave my mind at rest
But not to grieve or be sad
Thy sadness, my agonizing thud.

You allowed them, to lower me so deep
That in my bed, too narrow I couldn't move
And let the people walk, right on my chest.
Why punished me so, when I see, tears of love that proves
Yet forsake me, in my cold bed to rest;
Alone, and forever, in this endless dark,
That no one sees me, nor me to see the park.
And not refused this wretched place, where things that creep.

Languor, thus my soul, in the shadow of Hades
Allowed those roots, to frolic into thy body clutch
For I was not a perfect wife, that, I confess
As none on earth, could be as such.
But thank you, for all the love, I shared by your side,
And gladly, I took them all, to my last ride!

Oh! My beloved, how could you bear
To bury me so deep, I cannot see
The grass roots that grows upon me
The flower's smiles, its sweetness liked by bee,
Nor the sun to shun upon thee,
Nor the cherry blossoms in April morning
Or the spring's birds humming.
And all my lamentation, no one to share.
I can't feel the wind that passes by,
Nor blizzard's visits in winter's night
Or cyclones that blackens the sky
Nor be afraid, if it struck it's might
But still my soul of souls, will be in peace
Grant thy wish, I beg, if you please!

YOU WERE MINE FOR SO LONG

You were mine, for so long

And know, to me you do belong.

Yet consider how my heart felt

As our love now wilt.

For all my life humiliated by time

But will survive, if love sublime

Yet, if that love will come too late

The heart does act, its timely faith.

MR. WIND

When Mr. Wind will yawn
You'll get his scorn
Those lifeless twigs, will be blown.
To the streets, for human to tackle.

Autumn and winter's gone,
And spring arrives,
Squawking of ducks, can be heard,
As it passes your site.

Far and low as they make their flight
Back to their nest, where food is right.
So as the cardinals and raven on the trees,
Chirping songs, in the morning treats.

Southern wind, blows solemnly quiet
Kisses the flowers, wet by dew-drops at night.
Grass on the grounds, says hello,
Bows its head, as Mr. Wind blows low.

LITTLE PRINCESS OF THE VALLEY

Little Princess of the Valley

Wakes-up in the morning so early
.
Down the stairs running so merrily

Outside to pick white flowers by the alley.

Small foot-prints on the wet ground

Through the graveled path of the quiet land

On the vast meadows of flowers where she ran

Multicolored butterflies could be found.

The sun, humbled its face to the grove of nuts

Tiny hands gathered flowers of blue

Unalarmed as she run to the grassy field with morning dew

While the sun, now gliding on the roof of the hut

Suddenly remembered, breakfast time had past.

But fascinating flowers lure thy tiny hands to pick for last.

(For Inday)

CATTLEYA

To thy beauty we bestowed

Marveled in the tree top branches grow

And morning dew-drops kissed thy petals brow

As humid breeze keeps thyself low.

Large purple velvet hangs into the air

Cattleya, to its majestic beauty reign,

Showered by cold and misty rain

In virgin forest where she lay.

Fair as the maiden up in the cluster hide

Untouched by fingers, for no one could, by her side

The brown and green moss crowned the roots like hay

Its fragrance perfumed, the passing of night

While jealous sun, came rushing with its morning light.

PRECIOUS LITTLE LAMB

Oh! "Precious little lamb",

With skin of cotton-soft and smooth

Chinese silk, to thy compare that suits

To my precious, precious little lamb.

You wave tiny hands into the air

Bluish-fingers that is......., but so thick a hair

Snuggled in blanket of blue, with his monogram.

Opened his eyes, and so he tries,

To say hello to Mom and Dad.

He's big and healthy; that makes her very glad.

The skin that's fair, wrinkled like a bark,

And eyes that glitters, but so very dark.

(For my son John)

YOU'RE GOING AWAY

You're going away, away from me
No tears of joy, but misery
Away for so long, I can't be strong,
To suffer this anguish, my heart that was wrong.

I don't fear thee, for the happiness you may find
But the loneliness, you left me behind.
To lie on my cold bed, once, warmth by you
And woke-up in the still-night alone and blue.

I longed, your warmth, in frigid wintry night
The ground so white, no raven in sight.
The whistling breeze, that echoes to my heart
Siberian wind, blows my head apart.

Joy of my heart, when are you coming?
To wipe my tears that never cease falling
Dark-sunken eyes, humiliated by night,
Watching the night pass, with shred of fright.

I'm destined to wait, for you're coming late,
Outstretched arms, for you awaits,
Cried of my heart who loves so true
And honored thee, from head to toe.

AND WHEN I FEEL THE PAIN OF LONELINESS

And when I feel the pain of loneliness
Tears flooded to now, my ugly face,
Control is not at my command
For this melancholy heart is out of hand
To say I love you, burns even more.

To think where, my son, that I adore
Seven hundred darts, sticks in my heart
No relief with the passing of days, as we're apart.
You think your absence so short a time?
But for mother's heart the sun doesn't shine
No sorrows more painful on earth
Than the absence of a son, a mother's felt.

For you, it's but so temporary
My heart says, it's the beginning
Nevertheless, I know how you feel
Which we both have, the time, to steal
For these well be your boon
Triumphant days well come later on
My blithesome moments, is the glory of my son.

PRECIOUS BABY DOLL OF MY LIFE

In a freezing sunny day you came
Laid on my chest with tears of pain
A thud of joy and pity sucked my heart
To see my little Princess so hurt.

Lips were then and mottled
Cuddled by Daddy to keep her settled
Sorrows disappear, as the glory appears
Most wondrous moments of all.

No moments without joy
To see my lovely, lovely Princess with a toy
Morning and night, she talks to the clown
No cries could be heard all year round
But not a second I kept away from my sight
My precious, precious baby doll of my life,

As she grows older, the prettier she becomes
Face with glee in Mom's arms.
Voiceless tears, when mother not in sight;
Infinite joy, as she appears at the door.
In her blue denim hat, she rode in her cart
Out in the sun, in a beautiful flowering park.

THAT VISION

That vision uprooted my already caked brain
To be with those, whose lives crawled in the wheelchair.
What they see or hear, does not register in their dead brain

And look at you, like a black hole.

How did I come to this,
When it didn't reflect to my imagination;
In the years when I was moving like a wind.
And to be in this pit of horrid sorrows,
Was never .... in my conception.

What a false thought...........
To think that I was blessed in my life......
Surrounded with my loved ones,
And now, they are nowhere to be found
Lost, in the fulfillment of their happiness in life.
This cycle, I'm facing towards the end,
And them, in the middle.
How wonderful, so wonderful is life, when you're young
But horrible, terrifying, in ninety and one.

DESTINY

My love, I'm in deep sorrow
For I can't deliver tomorrow
The joy of love that we once felt
Thwarted by destiny, and compelled to dwell.
The mystery of life
Human can't deny
Love potion makes one's bride
Happiness was an oversight.
I'll be gratified to see thee leave;
If thy happiness is bestowed upon,
By some nymphs in the distant land.
Though malignant pain will gloat in my vein,
Relief to my conscience, I induce no pain
To my luscious love, my in capabilities thus deceived.

JULY

July, the moth you came,
Vacation, where I have been,
To see a stranger in suit of green,
Set my heart aflame.

That July morning, I met you
In green scrub by the window;
A smile of hello, though we don't know,
Turns out to be a lasting glow.

Nevertheless, the work drew us closer,
To friends and colleagues doesn't matter;
Only to hold them in wonder
What goes on, couldn't be better!
To help you, the happiness I felt,
And me by you, the glory you dealt!

THE INFANT

Spare me not thy sorrows,
For the endless morrows;
The sun is gliding
While you came out screaming.

To cradle you lay,
As soft as the hay
Thy sweet mother's smile,
Quenched thy hunger in time.

Sweet lullaby's she sings everyday,
Tiny ears listens with glee
Fuss, not when mother in site!
For she brings all goodness in life!

ANXIETY

Tears were falling
Heart was bursting
Sinking to the pit of unhappiness.
Frustrations coming;
Is this, the way to live?
I ask, but no answer.
Where could I go?
Whom could I ask?
Things were not clear,
And so are my feelings.
My heart, bursting of anxiety and fear!
Whom can I talk to?
Could time and patience be the answer?
Where could I, and how, I endure this pain.
I'm losing my strength, my confidence, my trust!
To myself, and to the people around me.
Alas! I could not say or ask..........
Is there a light behind this dark clouds?

GLORY ON THE OCEAN FLOOR

I live in the ocean floor
Corals my garden
Reefs my door.

I frolic with star fish
And fight with the sharks
Crawfish is my dish
My scales give light in dark.

I travel far and deep
To discover new things
Things myself enjoy, and keep.

A MOTHER IN PAIN

Oh, children I'm sorry
Your Mom is a worry
Not worth a penny
Seems to be her destiny.

She do you no good
As it has been told
Rotten mother as she
Had to flee.

So children, be good.
Follow your code.
Good children of Eden
Are welcome in heaven!

And when she is gone,
As swept as the sun;
Don't forget her teachings,
For that, will be your blessings.

THE ACCEPTABLE CHANGE

Lay not your hand on my cold flesh,
Nor your lips on my ashen face
Never to mistake, I need your warm embrace,
And smell sweet aroma of thy hair so fresh.

Now I seldom hear your voice,
To stay here was not my choice;
Neither you nor I voted
But God, in heaven has noted.

Where's the laughter I use to hear,
Not hearing them makes me despair;
And wake in early morning's glare
To find my waiting princess on her chair.

HAIL TO THE KING

Hail, to the King!
Who's smart and keen
Bright as the sun
That ruled his kingdom with fun.
Brilliant boy has been
Grow-up kind, not mean.
But the King is bound to shout
As his temper reach out.

The King is mad and furious
When laws and rules are not glorious;
Thunder footsteps you'll hear,
Be cautious, lightning is in the air.
Hide to the corner
Hide to the cellar
His fury will go that far.

Keep in mind, sisters and brothers
Of what you may say to father
Words could be dealt with belt;
That blazed, as you wilt.
Good manners had been the rule,
That we followed from the day we crawl,

Make mistakes and you will get
As the King, your father makes his fit!

When the storm died down,
Someone, to take the place of a clown,
Amiable face showed to daddy
Complement by his cherished baby!
Even the King has its own weakness;
As Samson was lured with a kiss,
So as the invincible Lord of the House
Has fallen to the kiss of his little mouse!

THE NOISY CREEK

By the noisy creek we met one day
Knowing not my name, nor you to me.
But we enjoyed each other's company,
And that we do it day-by-day.

By the noisy creek, we sat down side-by-side
We soaked our feet, by that cold water's glide
Down by the distance water creeks,
Passing our front with a slick!

How you laughed when I stumble on a crab,
Whose two claws high up for grab,
Then ran away to hide;
From the mighty tide.

You hold my hand, and help me cross the bank
The water creaking as it sinks.
Down it glide, and mixes with the tide;
Where cat fish took a quick dive.

By the noisy creek, we wait each other
To say hello, was not a bother.
We looked with joy and innocent faces,
No leeway of feeling, has its trace

For long a time that you were gone.
By the noisy creek I know not one.
The water flows as yester years
By the tree's bosom, I sank with tears.

PRECIOUS LOVE

Now, only worms roam on my face,
No fear of loneliness that come to me.
Noble Lord escape, yet could be trace;
By King Hades, so thy come to thee.
No laughter felt, on my rigid self,
Nor agonies, (of pain) that I once felt;
But forced to contempt 'til I wilt!
No sorrows seen on my ashen face.

Forsake not the memories we shared,
Of the precious love, I carried in my tomb.
As earthly life, was so declared
So short in time, but not to gloom,
For only bodies that decay
Not the precious love you promised in May.

NAIVENESS

You took the elevator which closes its door
And stop abruptly, on the fifth floor
Read the direction the lady give!

Walking alone in a narrow hallway,
Looking at the numbers printed at the doors
Confident to thy self to find the right way
White shoed feet, standing by the wall.

At the disk you approach a lady without a smile,
"Madame", (you said) am I in the floor to which I belong?
For I couldn't stand the pain I suffered so long.
Yes, you are, but you've to wait a mile!

IF I MAY DIE AHEAD OF TIME

If I may die ahead of time
That time so young embrace my life
Anoint me not with oil
But bathe me in perfume I do desire!

As I lay sleeping forever
Dressed in my most luxurious
Of white, lazy gown, so soft,
That will comfort me in my
Everlasting sleep.

THICK WALL OF LONELINESS

These thick wall of loneliness
I dare my life to live
Though pain encroached my heart
Yet, satisfaction gratifies my needs.

What more pain can a woman have
To see him with a woman not too smart!
A venom sting into my heart
When he kissed his lady love.

I denied my life, liberty and enthusiasm
And buried myself in a small darkened room!
Content in the lullaby of loneliness
Where tears and sorrows awaits.

JAPANESE WAY

Japs shouts of Hiroshima?
The devil is America!
Refused to know what evil they did;
Hundreds and millions of civilians dead!

Infants tossed to air, landed at their sword
Tied parents looked, can't say a word.
Young girls and women raped and killed!
While trees witnessed, to the men they killed.

Women and children hack
Bayonet at the back!

They came without warning,
Bull legged criminal Japs in the morning.
Heavy boots marching on the streets,
Run for your life, or you're a dead meat!

Farmers hanged on the trees
With tongues up to their knees.

Answer to questions, or they cut your tongue
Right or wrong, you'll still be hanged.

People forced to a timed-bombed church
As soldiers in Bataan on death march!

Americans were tortured to death,
Prisoners feed with cat and dogs meat
Waiting for McArthur to come,
As Truman ordered atom-bomb!

"Hiroshima here we come"
Cried the soldiers with the bomb!

Now hands on their heads,
Americans on the lead
They swallowed their pride,
So they will survive.

Decades past, to regain their lust
Monkey business with Americans
Congress are not blind, but refused to see;
Only to act, when we sank to the sea!!

(This poem is dedicated to those who died in the Philippines
During WWII)

CHRISTMAS

Christmas seasons
Has lots of reasons
To enjoy His birth,
Right here on earth.

Bells rings, here and there,
Everyone has merry cheers.
Joyous songs in the air,
Could be heard everywhere.

Children gather around
Santa making his rounds.
Close your eyes, and don't peep.
Through the chimney he'll creep.

Christmas breeze so bleak,
Fat goose in the lake.
Thick snow on the ground,
Fun to fool around.

VILLAGE LIGHT

Village light,
So calm and bright;
Various colors of lanterns shown,
With the skies beneath the moon.

Lanterns hanged at window sill,
Different shapes and motifs as the tell
Christmas winds, blowing its tail
People dreams of peace will never fail!

Oh, village light,
So calm and bright.
The cold December breeze,
Set our mind at rest.

Lanterns of blue, red, and orange that gleam,
Stars and comets as it may seem;
The sign for the coming of the King,
Is the joy of Christmas, it brings.

That light you see afar,
Only but the replica of a star.
And yet, the closer you look,
It's a symbol, we all took.

THE LONELY CROW

Oh, lonely crow that has no friends, but foe.
Sat way up high, at the cable wire
Watching, watching, the passers-by!
Its heart felled with loneliness that sets afire!

He shakes its folded wings, left to right
What discomfort this cold breeze to my eyes?
He wiggled his tail from left to right,
Find no comfort on the passing sight.

What could I do.....? Oh, nature I implore,
The passing of time, my heart aches even more.
And yet, I can't think of what morning brings,
But only to hope for the coming of spring!

THE CONTEST

Music is what we love to hear,
Loud and low to our very ear.
Keys to the pianos, strings to guitars,
Watch the fingers not go far.

Here comes the strict and wicked judge
To his rules you do abide.
To be his chosen is hard to do,
Bow low before you go.

Results is about to be read
Anxiety and shame is in your head.
To get first prize is what you aim,
Get no honor is but a shame!

Here's what to do in this situation,
Accept the facts in its condition.
Win or loss doesn't need consolation,
But man is known for its destruction!

TIME STOLE MY BABY

My baby with sweet angelic smile
Thick black hair straight up high
Dark eyes sparkling bright.
My sweet, sweet apple pie.
On his chest a blue ribbon tie.

Tiny toes straight in file
Small fingers touched my lips
Gratifies and console my chest.

No cries but laughter each day that comes
In the crib he stays quiet and calm
Times of hunger no shriek or bellow
But quietly waiting in his blanket so yellow.

How many a time I remember
How quick to put him in slumber
In that soft bed he lies.

But now, I turned around and see
I could not know, when I hear him coo
Thunder voices vibrates the walls
Heavy footsteps could dig a hole.

I looked up and was surprised
Big shadow shun to my eyes
And hug me with an iron arms
But smile to the sweetest charm.

COLUMBUS

I, the captain of the ship
To the sea that doesn't move, we crept
My men so tired
No ocean wind
Water so blue, no birds in sight.

For months, no land but ocean
Mammoth waves pushed us through
Or sunk to ocean floor below;
For sea monsters feast.

Oh! Holy Spirit come to thy rescue
Lead us to the land we never knew
With treasure to discover
Spices and herbs perfumed the air.

Me, Columbus, history will tell
To Herald Spain, whose ships that sail
Unknown lands we go, no one could tell
And to my Queen my life to spare.

AS I WAIT FOR YOU

As I wait for you, love
In that freezing and gloomy day
That corner streets; love,
Where no one wants to stay
For winds blow you away.

But to wait for you, love
Is my most exciting day.
The pleasure my heart could feel,
Like those people dancing in reel!
In that cold, freezing day.

BIRD'S WISHES

Oh! Creatures, big and small,
Some are lucky they are tall,
Dear little birdie wishes to fly,
But small wings couldn't go that high.
Poor little me, won't stop wishing,
'til the day I'll get the blessings!

Denies to wish, thyself condemn.
To wish not, is a problem.
To wish for is a trouble.
One couldn't win to its control.
Reaching them, would be wonderful.

I may be a birdie who can't reach the sky,
But I'm happy that I could fly.
Some creatures big, but stayed on the ground,
Can't see the view of its great town!
One could only wish, what they can't get
And should be happy what they can beat.

Poor little me, will find a way,
And not leave my life astray.

Life is fragile to all living things
And birds depend on their wings.
Those creatures that fly so high,
Reaches Olympus that touches the sky,
Were very, very, very,......LUCKY!

MY NATIVE LAND

Far in the Orient Seas
A land of greed
By Spain in deed.

For centuries was ruled
As histories fore told
By the greedy Spain
Puts the rights in vain.

Eighteen hundred sixty-one,
Born a great Khan
Risen rebellion
Cuts heads in a million.

Save your sin
From the *Fraile* of Spain
Or you'll find yourself,
In garrote.

Spanish language was forbidden
Natives were forsaken
Jewels, money and crops

93

Sent to Spain by raft.

Now, five hundred years had gone,
When Magellan was killed in Mactan;
Who aimed to kill Lapu-Lapu,
But 'was time to pay his due!

SAMPAGUITA

Sampaguita, how sweet a flower,
Jasmine is not to thy compare
For sweetness in its petals were
Dainty as it looks, that is so rare.

As morning sets its smiling face,
That you are eager to embrace
Your snowy petals beautiful than lace;
An honor to hold and thanks to thy grace.

Dear, Sampaguita fragrance you could tell,
A maiden's joy to be compared;
To thy beauty one would like to steal,
Is your wonder, no one could bear.

THE UNREACHABLE

How do I feel……..,
Looking up the grass that grow
I couldn't touch nor see its glow
Nor feel the fresh air that passes through.
People don't care,
What's beneath the earth under thy foot.
Nor think who's looking up without pursuit
Or, who's lying down on the bedded roots.

Yet, in my solitude……..
I always could remember
That one song in September
That easily put you in slumber.

I hear no buzzing of the bee,
Or is it the ringing of my ear?
My mouth is sealed no complaints to hear
As I used to do when I was there!

Now in my tomb………..,
Contained with infinite solitude,
No gloat for merriment nor humorous mood,
But tranquility is found in this servitude.

WHAT A JOY

A joyous song
For a precious jewel
Most precious
Priceless, loveliest;
Sing a lovely song
Sing a lullaby
To a precious love.

A beautiful song
Songs of merriment
For the jewel of love
I felt……….
Infinite landscape of joy.

My yearnings….
Granted!
Lovely, a lovely song……
For the creature of love
Joy, sweet joy
He's coming!

Drink, celebrate……..!
Thank Thee
Celebrate with songs

Songs to the Creator
Songs for creation
Joyous, lovely song
Thanksgiving songs.

What, a joy..........
In mother's heart
Song for the mother;
Song for the son.
Joyous songs
Loudest songs
In his coming.

PHILIPPINES, THE MISTAKEN TREASURE

Islands, no were in the mind of Spain
Knowledge of navigation so vain.
Conquistadors　with minds of greed
Collection of booty, all in their heads.

In search for spices, across the world
Traveled so far in deep ocean folds
Calculations inaccurate, and reliably wrong
Destined to India, that will take them long.

Rowing of ships, days not accounted
Reached in those islands, natives were busted.
Traveled through typhoons, hurricanes on its best
Lost hope of reaching, to the island to rest.

Months in the sea that feel like years
Persistence and well, tormented with fears.
Ocean's demons serpents and monsters
Not relieve with prayers, known to be human eater.

For at last they reach the islands
No gold nor spices drop on their hands
Forced the natives to give them gold

And to accept, their souls to be sold.

Now they accepted such religion
They found themselves in the dungeon.
Lands and animals were taken
And some ended in garrote.

WHAT IS THE ANSWER

Death, the joyous thing
That life could bring.
No pains nor sorrows
Could bring in the burrows.

Life is mean.
Treat people vain.
Death will stop,
And let memories hop.

No hope for the wicked,
It has been accepted.
As long as you live,
Troubles you can't upheave.

So, people who are bore
Miseries that life implore;
Take a good step
Life shouldn't slip!

PICKLES AND HONEY

Your lips taste like pickles in the jar,
It's a quick change by far
For only yesterday it tasted like honey
Whatever changed you, my love I know not me.

For so long, we enjoyed each other
Promises not to find another.
That love was young and blooming
Like stars in the skies that's beaming.

Wait, not so long and hold your breath,
The air anguish buried beneath
For you have taken for granted
That my love was never wanted.

So long, my love, as we part now
For you have broken our vows
But when your sourness changes to honey,
I'll be waiting for you like a mummy.

HOW DO I LOVE THEE

I love thee from deep within.
Not the physical structure that looks so keen,
But the inside of you;
One looks into view.

Your eyes reveals of many ideas that is…….
No one could miss, without a hiss
That looks in thy eyes Aristotle has in his brain,
Could pour and wet the mind in dry terrain.

I don't look for earthly beauty as you know,
But the intellectual power that I saw
Thine eyes speak, language philosophers could read.
Yet laymen see it greed!

Once, you told me, beauty, not what one sees
Man could die but forever will not free;
From the soul and body that once owned,
That nature's made it stronger than its bone.

Why do I love thee as much,
For not material things could bring as such!
In the years that we love each other,
Binds our soul and body mightier than ever.

Don't get me wrong that I don't get mad,
For madness is within human when they are sad.
Nevertheless, our love is strongly bounded;
And forever we could not be parted.

CLOUDS

Clouds come in cluster
Gliding smoothly up in the sky,
Raising groups, but not as high
If you run, you can be faster
Like those white clouds in a cluster.
Looked up to the clouds, from the ground you lie
You can't stop but give a big sigh!
When night comes, the sky looks brighter.

That nightly skies awaiting for morning sun.
Immobile clouds cluster from beyond
Patiently waiting the clear dusk of dawn.
When morning sun has just begun;
White clouds scattered like a magic wand
While crimson clouds, thy beauty is so grand.

SONGS TO ALMA MATER

Songs to Alma Mater we left behind
Songs to those years we shared in tears and laughter.
Language, we learned to speak that has remained in our
tongue.
Songs to the food at times too hard to swallow,
That pinched our hearts and make us mellow
But nevertheless, we struggle
Those strict rules we endure
As supervisors, love to see you crawl.
Songs to our poor patients that never question our capabilities
Song to our dear principal, whose perching looks besiege us
And to those melancholic nights, we cried 'til tears refuse to fall;
Popular song, the radio blasting as we prepare for morning
march!
Songs to Bohol's beautiful beaches, its green and chocolate hills
Breathing within ourselves the freshness of its air.
Songs to the Republic of BOHOL, with its friendly faces;
Millions of songs for the Nightingale of '68
But we sang: Hurry! To the weekends escapades when we are
caught empty handed?
Whether or not, we are free to leave
Our Alma Mater, will grave.

Farewell songs ruptured our hearts
To our Alma Mater, we depart.
Songs to the doctors whose kindness lift the pain of the days
More songs we sang to the unfortunate ones,
Whose lives were shortened by time.
Songs for the success we've achieved on foreign land
Yet, in our hearts our dear Alma Mater never cease on calling.